HISTORY'S GREATEST RIVALS

THOMAS JEFFERSON Vs. JOHN ADAMS

FOUNDING FATHERS AND POLITICAL RIVALS

Ellis Roxburgh

Please visit our website, **www.garethstevens.com**.
For a free color catalog of all our high-quality books,
call toll-free 1-800-542-2595 or fax 1-877-542-2596.

Library of Congress Cataloging-in-Publication Data

Roxburgh, Ellis.
Thomas Jefferson vs. John Adams : founding fathers and political rivals / Ellis Roxburgh.
pages cm. — (History's greatest rivals)
Includes index.
ISBN 978-1-4824-4239-7 (pbk.)
ISBN 978-1-4824-4240-3 (6 pack)
ISBN 978-1-4824-4241-0 (library binding)
1. Jefferson, Thomas, 1743-1826—Friends and associates—Juvenile literature. 2. Adams, John, 1735-1826—Friends and associates—Juvenile literature. 3. Founding Fathers of the United States—Juvenile literature. 4. Presidents—United States—Biography—Juvenile literature. 5. United States—Politics and government—1775-1783—Juvenile literature. 6. United States—Politics and government—1783-1809—Juvenile literature. I. Title.
E332.2.R69 2016
973.4'6092—dc23

2015025567

Published in 2016 by
Gareth Stevens Publishing
111 East 14th Street, Suite 349
New York, NY 10003

For Brown Bear Books Ltd:
Editorial Director: Lindsey Lowe
Managing Editor: Tim Cooke
Children's Publisher: Anne O'Daly
Design Manager: Keith Davis
Designer: Lynne lennon
Picture Manager: Sophie Mortimer

Picture Credits: T=Top, C=Center, B=Bottom, L=Left, R=Right. Front Cover: Shutterstock: Nixx Photography background. US Navy: r, Whitehouse Historical Association: l. Brooklyn Museum: 38; Library of Congress: 7, 8, 11, 15, 23, 26, 31, 32, 33, 35, 39; National Portrait Gallery: 22; New York Historical Society: 22; Palace of Versailles: 20; Robert Hunt Library: 9, 12, 14, 16, 21, 24, 27, 28, 41; Shutterstock: D N Davis 25, Daniel M Silva 13; Thinkstock: Susan Law Canin 18, Paul Fries 37, Matthew Lee 36; Topfoto: The Granger Collecion 40; Trout Gallery: 34; United States Federal Government: 30; United States House of Representatives: 19; US National Archives: 17: US Navy: 29.

Manufactured in the United States of America

CPSIA compliance information: Batch #CW16GS. For further information contact Gareth Stevens, New York, New York at 1-800-542-2595.

CONTENTS

AT ODDS

THOMAS JEFFERSON

JOHN ADAMS

Thomas Jefferson (1743–1826) became the third president of the United States. He drafted the Declaration of Independence in 1776.

* **Jefferson came from Virginia and was a slave owner.**
* **Jefferson was tall and skinny, and known for not talking much.**
* **Jefferson was an idealist. He believed the future would always be better than the past.**
* **He saw the good in everyone and believed that people had a great capacity for change.**
* **Jefferson is celebrated as being one of America's greatest political figures.**

The second president of the United States, John Adams (1735–1826) was also one of the main supporters of American independence.

* Adams was a lawyer from Massachusetts. He defended British soldiers charged with shooting Americans in the Boston Massacre (1770).

* He was short and fat, and loved to talk.

* Adams believed that people always put themselves first, above what might benefit everyone in society.

* He was a realist who believed that people learned from the past.

* Adams has had a lower profile than some of the other Founders for the last 200 years.

CONTEXT

Thomas Jefferson and John Adams first met in 1775. The Revolutionary War had just begun as the American colonies tried to break their ties with their rulers in Great Britain.

The two men became friendly at the Second Continental Congress that met in Philadelphia in May 1775. Delegates from Britain's 13 American colonies gathered to discuss the revolution.

KING: King George III angered colonial Americans by refusing to listen to their complaints about unfair taxation.

Unhappy Colonies

At the time, the colonies were still ruled by Great Britain from London. They were subject to British laws and taxation. Americans had to trade exclusively with Great Britain, follow British customs, and pledge allegiance to the British king, George III. In exchange, Britain would protect the colonies from interference by other European powers or from clashes with hostile Native American tribes.

BOSTON: On March 5, 1770, British soldiers killed protestors in the so-called Boston Massacre.

War and Debt

The bond between the colonies and their rulers started to unravel after the Seven Years' War (1756–1763). This was principally a war between Britain and its European neighbor, France, but it affected most of the world. In North America, the British and their colonies fought against the French in Canada. This American part of the war was called the French and Indian War (1754–1763). Although Britain gained almost all of France's North American territory east of the Mississippi River, the war left the British heavily in debt.

> **"Facts are stubborn things; and whatever may be our wishes they cannot alter the state of facts and evidence."**

John Adams, defending British soldiers after the Boston Massacre, 1770

> “We have it in our power to begin the world over again.”

Thomas Paine talking about the Revolutionary War, 1776

Raising Taxes

To pay off its debts, the British parliament decided to tax the Americans more heavily. Between 1756 and 1775, parliament imposed numerous taxes, including taxes on tea and on printed documents. The new taxes met with opposition in America, particularly as colonial Americans were not represented in the British Parliament, so could not argue against the measures. In the face of protests led by New England, the British sent many more troops to America to try to restore order. Tensions rose between the British and the Americans, who called themselves Patriots. On April 19, 1775, the two sides clashed in the Battles of Lexington and Concord. The Revolutionary War had begun.

WAR: The first shots of the Revolutionary War were fired at Lexington on April 19, 1775.

CITY: Jefferson and Adams became friends in Philadelphia, where the Second Continental Congress met.

Until the first shots were fired, most Americans had hoped to resolve their differences with Britain. But after King George III failed to address their concerns, they felt they had no choice but to rebel.

Contrasting Experience

John Adams came from Massachusetts, where British soldiers had arrived in 1768 to keep the peace. In 1770 troops had opened fire on protestors in Boston, in what became known as the Boston Massacre. As a lawyer, Adams had defended the British soldiers who killed five people. Thomas Jefferson was from Virginia. Unlike Adams, he had few dealings with the Patriots of the revolutionary movement. He was from a leading family, however, so he was a significant figure at the Second Continental Congress.

THOMAS JEFFERSON

» PRIVILEGED UPBRINGING

Jefferson was an unlikely politician. He was painfully shy and preferred a quiet home life with his family to the noise of political life.

Jefferson was the son of a wealthy Virginia farmer and slave owner. Thomas trained as a lawyer although, unlike Adams, he did not enjoy the law. However, he used his earnings to build a magnificent home, Monticello, in Virginia, which he added to throughout his life.

Political Life

Between 1769 and 1775, Jefferson was a member of Virginia's legislative assembly, the House of Burgesses. By 1774, he was arguing and writing articles against British rule. His fluent writing led to his being the chief author of the Declaration of Independence in 1776.

PRIVILEGE: Jefferson was brought up in one of the leading families in Virginia.

HOME: Jefferson designed his own home at Monticello, which was originally built in 1772.

Minister in France

In 1784, the new United States Congress sent Jefferson to France to make trade deals. He lived in Paris, where he witnessed the start of the French Revolution of 1789. While in Paris, Jefferson also visited John Adams, who was based in London. The two men became closer friends. Recalled to America by George Washington, the first president, Jefferson became secretary of state in 1790; John Adams was the first vice president.

> "The only person Adams could associate with with perfect freedom and unreserve."

Abigail Adams on Thomas Jefferson

JOHN ADAMS

» A MAN OF PRINCIPLE

Adams was part of a Massachusetts political dynasty that included his cousin Samuel Adams and his son, John Quincy Adams.

ADAMS: John Adams was known throughout his life for sticking to his principles.

Like Jefferson, Adams trained as a lawyer. Unlike Jefferson, however, Adams loved the law and rose to become one of Boston's most senior lawyers. His defense of British soldiers after the 1770 Boston Massacre made him unpopular in Boston, but it reflected the unwavering strength of his principles. He put his dedication to the law above his personal feelings that the British soldiers had behaved badly.

A Reluctant Patriot

Adams had been involved in protests against British rule since they began. His cousin, Samuel, was one of the leaders of the Patriots in Boston. John, meanwhile, originally wanted to remain under British rule if Britain addressed the colonies' concerns. He changed his mind after the Revolutionary War began. Adams was responsible for raising money for the Patriots and equipping the army and navy.

HOME: Adams was born in 1735 in this modest wooden home in Braintree, Massachusetts.

Working in Europe

In 1778, Congress sent Adams to Paris to gain support from the French against the British. He returned there twice more. In 1783 he was one of three US representatives to sign the Treaty of Paris, ending the Revolutionary War. He became the first US ambassador to Britain in 1785, remaining in London until 1788. He had to endure a four-year absence from his beloved wife, Abigail, who remained in America while he was in Europe. During that time, Jefferson visited Adams often and the two men became close friends. They even made a tour of southern England together. On his return to America, Adams became the country's first vice president in the government of George Washington.

> "Profound in his vision and accurate in his judgment."
>
> **Thomas Jefferson on John Adams**

FRIENDS AND ALLIES

» JEFFERSON'S SUPPORTERS

Jefferson was devastated when his wife died. In later life, his close friends included some of the most important men of the age.

In 1772, Jefferson married a widow named Martha Wayles Skelton. The marriage transformed Jefferson's life. His childhood had not been particularly happy but with his wife and their children he discovered the happiness family life at home at Monticello could bring. When Martha died in 1782, after the birth of their youngest daughter, Lucy, Jefferson was devastated. He was happy to leave Monticello and escape to Europe to serve the United States.

WIFE: Martha Jefferson asked her husband not to marry again, and he never did.

Another Woman

In Europe, Jefferson was a close friend of John Adams' wife, Abigail. After Martha's death, Abigail invited Jefferson to visit her family more often. However, when Jefferson and Adams first fell out in 1791, she broke off contact with Jefferson. She resumed contact in

FRIEND: Benjamin Franklin, the writer and scientist, became good friends with Jefferson while in Paris.

1804, when she wrote to him about the death of his daughter, Mary, (known as "Polly"), who died when she was just 25 years old. However, when Jefferson talked about his political differences with her husband, Abigail broke off contact again.

Political Allies

Jefferson was admired by many of the politicians who helped found the United States. Jefferson himself admired Benjamin Franklin, the writer from Philadelphia. Franklin spent much of his time in Europe, raising support for the United States. The friends spent nine months together in Paris after Jefferson arrived there in 1784.

> "He is one of the choice ones of the Earth."

Abigail Adams on Thomas Jefferson, May 1785

A SMALL CIRCLE

» ADAMS' FAMILY AND FRIENDS

Adams relied on his family for support. However, he was known to have a short temper, which meant he was not always popular.

WIFE: Abigail Adams wrote many letters to her husband about political subjects and influenced his views.

Adams married Abigail Smith in 1764. They were third cousins. Abigail was known for her intelligence. She also found it easier to get along with other people than her husband. However, she gave Adams wise advice throughout his career before her death in 1818.

Adams was lonely when he was sent to Europe in 1785. Abigail stayed home, and they did not see each other again for four years.

Adams' other great support was his son John Quincy Adams, who became the sixth president of the United States in 1825. When John Adams argued with Thomas Jefferson in 1791 over Thomas Paine's book *The Rights of Man*, John Quincy Adams defended his father. He published an anonymous article in the newspapers in Boston

SON: John Quincy Adams became president in 1825. He was always a loyal supporter of his father.

under the name "Publicola." John Quincy Adams argued that Jefferson had misunderstood Paine's book.

Founding Doctor

John Adams' prickly personality meant that he had few close friends among the Founding Fathers. However, one of his most valued friends was Benjamin Rush, a physician from Philadelphia. It was Rush who finally reconciled Adams and Jefferson.

> "This illustrious patriot has ... scarcely his equal for abilities and virtue on the whole continent of America."

Benjamin Rush on John Adams, September 1776

LINES ARE DRAWN

» CREATING A NEW COUNTRY

The Second Continental Congress asked John Adams, Thomas Jefferson, and Benjamin Franklin to draft a declaration of independence.

Although the three men worked on the document together, Jefferson took the leading role. He had a reputation as an outstanding writer. In the Declaration of Independence, Jefferson spelled out his belief that the government's role was to commit America to the ideals of freedom and equality. He believed people were honorable, so the government did not need to play a big role in daily life.

IN CONGRESS, JULY 4, 1776.

The unanimous Declaration of the thirteen united States of America,

SIGNED: The Declaration of Independence was drafted by Thomas Jefferson, John Adams, and Benjamin Franklin.

John Adams disagreed. He believed people always became corrupted by power. Adams believed the best way forward was a government formed of three branches: the legislature, the executive, and the judiciary. Each branch of government would be balanced and

PRESENTATION: The US Constitution is adopted by the Constitutional Convention in September 1787.

controlled by the other two. For Jefferson, however, this had the effect of making the federal government too big and powerful.

> **"We hold these truths to be self-evident, that all men are created equal, that they are endowed by their Creator with certain unalienable Rights, that among these are Life, Liberty and the pursuit of Happiness."**

Thomas Jefferson, Declaration of Independence, 1776

Jefferson's View

After the end of the American Revolution, a new US Constitution was adopted on September 17, 1787. Both Adams and Jefferson were in Europe. But their differences about the shape of the United States were clear: Jefferson favored more state control while Adams wanted a strong federal government.

FRENCH REVOLUTION

FLASH POINT **» OVERTHROWING THE MONARCHY**

In 1789, France erupted into revolution. The French rose up against the king and formed a new republican government.

Thomas Jefferson was living in Paris when the French Revolution started. Jefferson saw the French uprising as evidence that ordinary people could run their own country without any need for a king. Even after the revolution entered a period called the "Terror" in 1790, when many thousands of people were executed—including King Louis XVI and Queen Marie Antoinette—Jefferson continued to support its aims. Unlike Jefferson, John Adams saw the revolution as proof that anarchy was never far away. The French Revolution convinced him further of the need for strong central government.

RIOTS: French citizens fight the army of King Louis XVI in the streets of Paris.

EXECUTION: King Louis XVI was executed on January 21, 1793.

A Divided Government

The French Revolution split George Washington's government. Jefferson was among the politicians who believed the Americans should support the new government in France. After all, the French had supported the Americans during the Revolutionary War against Britain. Jefferson became leader of the pro-French Democratic-Republican Party. Adams supported the Federalist Party. This party supported Britain, where the rulers were against the French Revolution. Unlike Jefferson, Adams greatly admired the British monarchy and nobility.

> "You are afraid of the one, I, of the few."

Adams to Jefferson about Jefferson's distrust of a king and his own distrust of the revolutionaries, 1787

THE RIGHTS OF MAN

FLASH POINT » A CONTROVERSIAL PUBLICATION

Following their disagreement over the French Revolution, Adams and Jefferson found their friendship strained by an unlikely dispute.

In 1791, the British author Thomas Paine wrote a book called *The Rights of Man*. It defended the ideas behind the French Revolution. Jefferson enjoyed Paine's book, as he explained in a letter to a printer in Philadelphia. Without Jefferson's knowledge, the printer included the letter as the introduction to an edition of the book. John Adams was offended. The "introduction" made it clear that Jefferson thought Adams' views on the French Revolution were mistaken.

RIGHTS: Paine argued that people had the right to overthrow a government that ruled poorly.

MAD: This American cartoon of Paine was entitled "Mad Tom." Like Adams, many Americans distrusted the author and his ideas.

Breaking Off Contact

Jefferson wrote Adams to explain what had happened. However, he only made things worse. Jefferson claimed that the real problem was not his opinions but those of "Publicola," a writer who appeared to defend Adams' views. "Publicola" was, in fact, Adams' son, John Quincy. What began as a minor disagreement ended with Adams breaking off all personal contact with Jefferson.

> "That you and I differ in our ideas of the best form of government is well known to us both."

Jefferson to Adams, July 17, 1791

JAY'S TREATY

FLASH POINT » AN UNSATISFACTORY TREATY

On November 19, 1794, the United States and Britain signed a treaty written by the US Secretary of Foreign Affairs, John Jay.

After the Revolutionary War and the independence of the United States, many issues remained unresolved between the Americans and their former colonial rulers, Great Britain. There were still British soldiers on US soil near the border with Canada, for example. What was known as Jay's Treaty aimed to resolve the issues between the two countries.

TREATY
OF
Amity, *Commerce*, and *Navigation*,
BETWEEN
HIS *BRITANNICK* MAJESTY
AND THE
UNITED STATES of *AMERICA*,
Signed at *London*, the 19th of *November*, 1794.

Published by Authority.

DIEU ET MON DROIT

LONDON:
Printed by EDWARD JOHNSTON, in *Warwick-Lane.*

TREATY: When Jay agreed to trade with Britain's colonies, many Americans objected.

The treaty agreed to the border between the United States and British-held Canada. It removed all British soldiers from what was now US territory. The British allowed the Americans to trade with their colonies in India and the Caribbean. In return, the Americans agreed to limit their cotton exports so as not to

LAND: Under Jay's Treaty, Britain removed its troops from US soil along the Ohio River next to Canada.

compete with Britain's cotton trade. Thomas Jefferson opposed the treaty. He did not want a special trading relationship with Britain. He said that a complete break with Great Britain was the only way to give the United States a chance at full independence.

An Alternative View

John Adams, however, supported the treaty. Like George Washington, he believed the United States should keep a close relationship with Britain. He made it clear that he admired the British system, with its monarchy and aristocracy. Adams believed the US system should eventually become something more like the British system.

> "Those who own the country ought to govern it."
>
> **John Jay, *Federalist Papers*, 1788**

ELECTION OF 1796

FLASH POINT » POLITICAL CONTEST

The election of 1796 was the first contested presidential election. In both previous elections, George Washington had run unopposed.

By the time of the 1796 election, politics was dominated by two parties. John Adams stood on behalf of the Federalist Party, which stood for strong central government and close ties with Britain. Meanwhile, Jefferson stood for the Democratic-Republican Party, which favored stronger state government and close relations with France. Adams won the election, becoming the second president. The rules of the time required that Jefferson became vice president, even though he was from a different party. Despite falling out over Thomas Paine's book in 1791, Adams asked Jefferson to join his cabinet to shape foreign policy. Even though he was vice president, Jefferson refused.

PRESIDENT: This engraving commemorates Adams' single term as president.

The Rift Deepens

Adams faced an immediate problem in foreign affairs. His cabinet wanted to go to

VICTORY: This banner celebrates Jefferson's defeat of Adams in the presidential election of 1800.

war with the French, who were raiding US merchant ships. The French were angry that the United States favored Britain in its trade deals. Adams agreed that France was an enemy of the United States, but he realized the country could not afford a war. Jefferson also wanted to avoid war—but for different reasons. He still supported the French Revolution, and believed the United States should help a nation that had helped his own nation during the Revolutionary War. He saw no reason for the United States to go to war with France.

> **"A man whose mind is warped by prejudice and so blinded by ignorance as to be unfit for the office he holds."**

John Adams on Jefferson, 1797

UNDECLARED WAR

FLASH POINT » FIGHTING THE FRENCH

In 1798, tensions between the United States and France finally flared up in the waters of the Caribbean Sea.

REVOLT: The Federalists argued that the French Revolution meant the United States no longer had to repay loans from the old French government.

The United States had refused to pay back loans it had borrowed from France during the Revolutionary War. The Americans argued that the French monarchy had made the loan, not the republic created after the French Revolution. Meanwhile, the French were angered by Jay's Treaty. They believed it gave their enemy, Britain, a trading advantage with the United States.

French ships started to attack American vessels in the Caribbean. They seized goods the United States was trading with Great Britain. When officials met in Paris in April 1798 to discuss the problem, the French demanded a large amount of money to restore diplomatic relations with the Americans. The result was

CLASH: The USS *Constellation* (left) captures the French ship *Insurgente* on February 9, 1799.

the so-called Quasi-War. From July 1798 until September 1800, the United States and France fought an undeclared war at sea.

War or Not?

Adams was being drawn by his government toward a formal war. Jefferson still sided with France. He was angry that Adams did not stand up more strongly to those calling for war. In the end, Adams sent a second delegation to France that made a peace deal. But it appeared that he had given in to French pressure. That ruined his reputation, and his political career was badly damaged.

> **"At present, there is no more prospect of seeing a French army here, than there is in Heaven."**
>
> **John Adams, October 22, 1798**

DIVISIVE ACTS

FLASH POINT » **SILENCING CRITICISM**

Jefferson and Adams' relationship reached another low when Adams passed the Alien and Sedition Acts later in 1798.

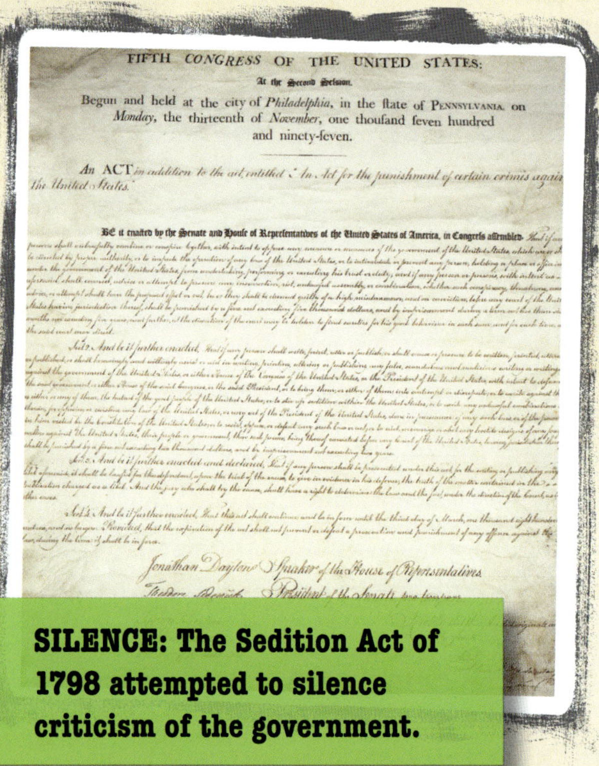

FIFTH CONGRESS OF THE UNITED STATES:
At the Second Session.
Begun and held at the city of *Philadelphia*, in the state of PENNSYLVANIA, on *Monday*, the thirteenth of *November*, one thousand seven hundred and ninety-seven.

An ACT *in addition to the act entitled "An Act for the punishment of certain crimes against the United States."*

BE it enacted by the Senate and House of Representatives of the United States of America, in Congress assembled, ...

Jonathan Dayton Speaker of the House of Representatives

SILENCE: The Sedition Act of 1798 attempted to silence criticism of the government.

The acts introduced four laws that aimed to limit the activities of foreigners in the United States. The supporters of the acts wanted to protect the country from foreign-born people who criticized the government. Now foreign-born people could be forced to leave the country and any immigrant had to live in the United States for 14 years before he or she could become a US citizen. Under the Sedition Act it was forbidden to publish anything that the government considered to be untrue. Many people thought that was an attempt by Adams to silence Jefferson and his supporters.

A Difficult Position

Although the laws were passed by Adams, Jefferson opposed them. He found himself in the difficult position of opposing the president

MOCKERY: This Federalist cartoon shows Jefferson and the Devil trying to pull down the federal government.

while serving in his administration. In response, Jefferson and his friend, James Madison, drafted what became known as the "Kentucky and Virginia Resolutions." Jefferson and Madison argued that Adams' new laws broke the US Constitution. In addition, they argued states should be allowed to nullify federal laws they believed to be illegal under the terms of the Constitution.

> **"Were it left to me to decide whether we should have a government without newspapers, or newspapers without a government, I should not hesitate to prefer the latter."**

Thomas Jefferson to John Adams, 1800

ELECTION OF 1800

FLASH POINT **» THE FINAL SPLIT**

Jefferson and Adams went head to head again in the election of 1800. This time, Jefferson won and their friendship was at an end.

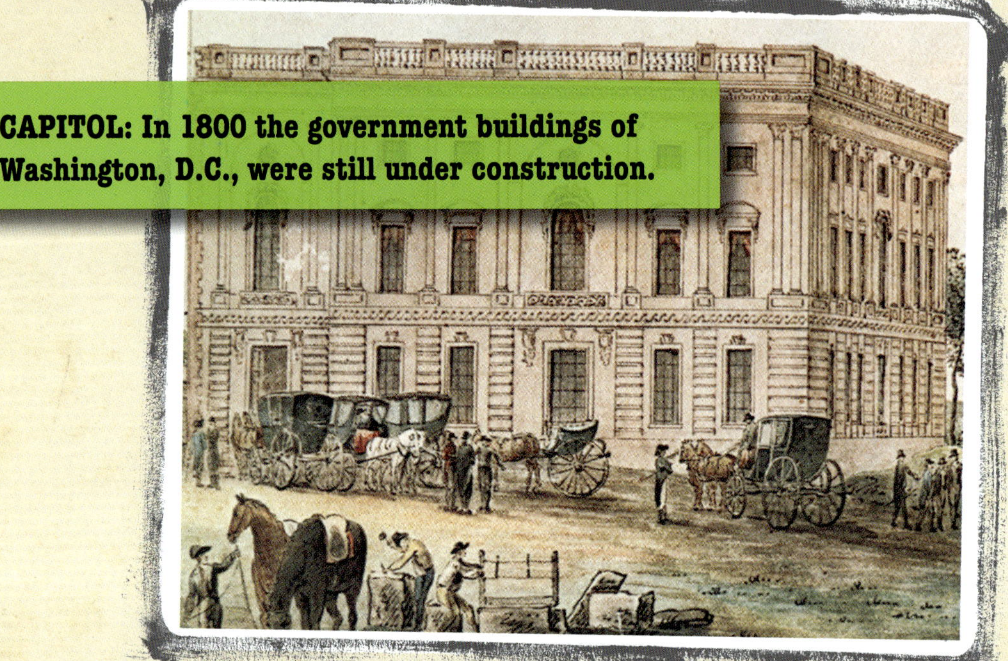

CAPITOL: In 1800 the government buildings of Washington, D.C., were still under construction.

The views of Jefferson and Adams were still far apart. But while the Democratic-Republicans unified behind Jefferson, Adams' Federalist Party were busy arguing with one another. Jefferson and fellow Democratic-Republican Aaron Burr got the same number of votes in the electoral college, but the House of Representatives awarded the victory to Jefferson.

In the last weeks of his presidency, Adams desperately tried to reorganize the judicial system. He created many Federalist "midnight judges," named because Adams was appointing them

COMPARISON: This cartoon compares Jefferson (right) in an unfavorable way to George Washington, the first US president.

until the very end of his term. The move irritated Jefferson. He saw the appointments as Adams meddling in his presidency.

End of a Friendship

Adams left Washington, D.C., and returned to Massachusetts right after the election. He did not attend Jefferson's inauguration. He did not even leave a note of congratulations for the new president. The two former friends and colleagues had no further contact with each other for more than a decade.

> **"Well, I understand that you are to beat me in this contest."**
>
> **John Adams to Thomas Jefferson, 1800**

RUSH'S DREAM

FLASH POINT » **ENDING THE DIVISIONS**

Thomas Jefferson served two terms as president. During that time, he and Adams broke off contact. This silence continued into their retirement.

The Philadelphia physician Benjamin Rush was one of the leading Founding Fathers. As a friend of both Jefferson and Adams, he was deeply troubled that the two men had lost their friendship. In 1809, Rush had a dream in which he saw Jefferson and Adams becoming friends again. He dreamed that Adams wrote to Jefferson, congratulating him on his retirement from the White House. Rush was so inspired that he wrote a letter about his dream to Adams, who was living quietly in Quincy with his family.

DOCTOR: Benjamin Rush helped to found the modern science of psychiatry, or mental health.

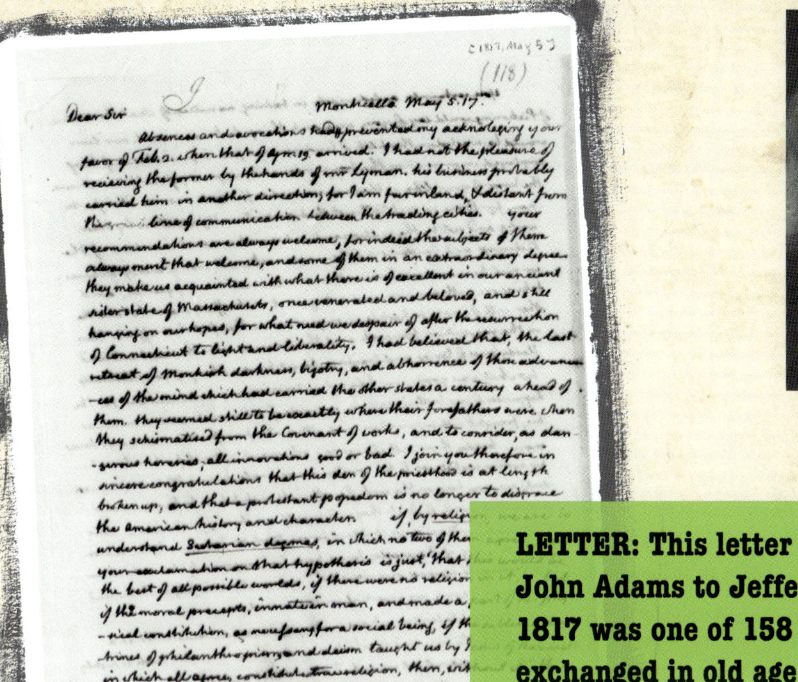

c1817, May 5

(118)

Dear Sir Monticello May 5. 17.

Absences and avocations had prevented my acknoleging your favor of Feb. 2. when that of Apr. 19. arrived. I had not the pleasure of recieving the former by the hands of mr Lyman. his business probably carried him in another direction, for I am far inland, & distant from the line of communication between the trading cities. your recommendations are always welcome, for indeed the subjects of them always merit that welcome, and some of them in an extraordinary degree. they make us acquainted with what there is of excellent in our ancient sister state of Massachusets, once venerated and beloved, and still hanging on our hopes, for what need we despair of after the resurrection of Connecticut to light and liberality. I had believed that, the last retreat of Monkish darkness, bigotry, and abhorrence of those advances of the mind which had carried the other states a century ahead of them. they seemed still to be exactly where their forefathers were when they schismatised from the Covenant of works, and to consider, as dangerous heresies, all innovations good or bad. I join you therefore in sincere congratulations that this den of the priesthood is at length broken up, and that a protestant popedom is no longer to disgrace the American history and character. if, by religion

understand Sectarian dogmas, in which no two of them

your exclamation on that hypothesis is just, 'that

the best of all possible worlds, if there were no religion

if the moral precepts, innate in man, and made a

-sical constitution, as necessary for a social being, if the

-trines of philanthropism and deism taught us by

in which all agree, constitute true religion, then, without

would be, as you again say, 'something not fit to be nam

President Adams.

37402

LETTER: This letter from John Adams to Jefferson in 1817 was one of 158 they exchanged in old age.

A Reconciliation by Post

A couple of years after Rush dreamed that Adams and Jefferson became friends again, the dream came true. On January 1, 1812, Adams addressed his first letter to Jefferson in years. He wished Jefferson a happy new year. Adams sent the letter to Jefferson's home at Monticello. A month later he received a letter from Jefferson. Soon the letters between the two men started up again. Over the following years they exchanged 158 letters before their deaths. In their letters they explored why they had fallen out and discussed their ideas about the nation.

> "You and I ought not to die, before We have explained ourselves to each other."
>
> **John Adams to Thomas Jefferson, July 15, 1813**

JEFFERSON'S OLD AGE

» LOYAL TO THE REVOLUTION

Jefferson always believed that his falling out with John Adams could have been avoided, despite their contrasting political views.

Jefferson always saw the Revolutionary War as being merely the start of the great political change needed in America. He believed strongly that the United States needed to create its own future by breaking with its past. That was one reason he believed France to be a more important ally than Britain, America's former colonial ruler. He also continued to support the French Revolution, even after it became violent. He thought it was necessary for the French to break with their past.

MEMORIAL: This statue of Jefferson stands in the Jefferson Memorial in Washington, D.C.

Jefferson knew that John Adams did not agree with any of his views. But he valued Adams' opinions and had missed their exchanges of letters after they fell out. Jefferson believed that no political differences should be able to destroy a long friendship.

MONUMENT: Jefferson's is one of the faces of four presidents carved into Mount Rushmore in South Dakota.

Renewing A Friendship

Jefferson served as president from March 1801 until March 1809. He retired to Monticello, where he spent his time reading and running his estate. In 1811, one of his neighbors visited Adams. The man told Jefferson that Adams missed him. Jefferson asked Benjamin Rush to try to help the men become friends again. Rush persuaded Adams to write to Jefferson. Their political rivalry was over.

> "Different conclusions we had drawn from our political reading."

Thomas Jefferson explains to Abigail Adams what had separated him from her husband, June 13, 1804

QUIET RETIREMENT

» OLD AGE IN QUINCY

His defeat in the 1800 presidential election left Adams shattered. He left Washington, D.C., without attending Jefferson's inauguration.

Adams remained at home in Quincy, Massachusetts, during Jefferson's two terms as president. He spent his time reading, working on his autobiography, and writing to his political allies. In 1812, he was persuaded by Benjamin Rush to write to Jefferson. The two men were reconciled. For the next 14 years, the two men wrote to one another regularly (Adams wrote more frequently but Jefferson's letters were longer).

PORTRAIT: Adams became a widower when his wife Abigail died in 1818.

INHERITANCE: Adams lived long enough to see his son, John Quincy Adams, become president in 1825.

Going Over the Past

In their letters, the two men discussed politics and wrote about their respective terms as president. Adams came to understand that he and Jefferson had not been as far apart politically as he had thought during the 1790s and 1800s. Adams in particular wrote about their past disagreements, but the two men were able to avoid falling out again. Their renewed friendship brought them much pleasure in their final years.

> "I always loved Jefferson, and still love him."

Adams on Jefferson before their reconciliation

AFTERMATH

» CONTRASTING REPUTATIONS

On July 4, 1826, Jefferson and Adams died within hours of each other. It was the 50th anniversary of American independence.

Since their deaths, Jefferson's reputation has tended to overshadow that of Adams. Jefferson wrote his own words for his gravestone in Monticello. It reads, "Here was buried Thomas Jefferson, Author of the Declaration of American Independence, of the Statute of Virginia for Religious Freedom and the Father of the University of Virginia."

FUNERAL THOUGHTS,

EXCITED BY THE DEATH OF

JOHN ADAMS

AND

THOS. JEFFERSON,

ON THE FOURTH OF JULY 1826, THE JUBILEE OF INDEPENDENCE.

☞President ADAMS was born Oct. 19, 1735; and President JEFFERSON, April 2, 1743.

" *What mean ye by this service?*" This question, it was foreseen, would, in the promised land of Canaan, be addressed by children to their parents, when they should yearly celebrate the Passover; and thus commemorate their merciful and miraculous deliverance from tyranny and bondage. The question may as naturally arise *what mean the "Funeral honours,"* of which so much is spoken and published?—With reference to living rulers, whom Paul denominates God's ministers, he saith "Render therefore to all their dues; tribute to whom tribute is due; custom to whom custom; fear to whom fear; honour to whom honour." But how can we render honours to the dead? or how can the dead receive honours? The benefit not of the dead, but of the living; the glory, not of the creature, but of the Creator, are the highest motives which can be proposed in performing Funeral honours.

When it is asked therefore, What mean the "Funeral honours?" what mean the solemn tolling of bells; the various badges of mourning; the funeral processions; the vessels in the harbour with their colours at half-mast; the stores and mechanic shops closed, on a day which is not the Sabbath? What mean the crowded assemblies to attend to funeral prayers and elegies, and anthems? The answer is, two men, whom God in his Providence made instrumental of procuring and perpetuating national blessings, have departed this life. It is believed the public good of the nation may be promoted by some peculiar "Funeral honours," and particularly by delineating their characters. And while we mourn for the men as Patriots and Benefactors, we are bound especially to give glory to God, as the source of all our blessings; and to humble ourselves for our individual and national sins. "Humble yourselves therefore in the sight of the Lord, and he shall lift you up.—Whatsoever ye do, do all to the glory of God." James iv. 10.—1 Cor. x. 31.

The BIBLE itself, the holy Book of GOD, fur-

old, and they buried him in the border of his inheritance, in Timnath-Serah, which is in Mount Ephraim, on the north side of the hill Gaash."

Samuel was instrumental of delivering the nation of Israel from the dominion of the Philistines. A great victory gained by his means, was commemorated by a monument. "And Samuel took a stone and set it between Mispeh and Shen, and called the name of it Ebenezer, saying, "*Hitherto hath the Lord helped us.*" "And Samuel died; and all the Israelites were gathered together, and lamented him, and buried him in his house at Ramah." 1 Sam. vii. 12, and xxv. 1.

When Saul and Jonathan, the first king of Israel, and his son, died, king David composed an Elegy, which was probably sung on the occeson: "The beauty of Israel is slain upon the high places; how are the mighty fallen! Saul and Jonathan were lovely and pleasant in their lives, and in their death they were not divided." 2 Sam. 1.

Will not the American people say, that these words are with peculiar force, applicable to the illustrious dead, who departed this life on the memorable 4th of July, 1826?

Jehoiada, the Chief Priest in Jerusalem, was distinguished both for his patriotism and piety. His influence in delivering the nation from tyranny and idolatry, was conspicuous; and a peculiar respect for his memory was manifested. "They offered burnt offerings in the house of the Lord continually, all the days of Jehoiada. But Jehoiada waxed old, and was full of days, when he died; an 130 years old was he when he died; and they buried him in the city of David, among the kings, because he had done good in Israel both towards God and towards his house." 2 Ch. xxiv. 14, &c.

Josiah, king of Judah, was a pious patriot, and manifested his patriotism by his remarkable and persevering efforts to root out idolatry, and to destroy the abounding iniquities of the land, and by promoting the worship of the true God. Being

BROADSIDE: This pamphlet mourned the deaths of Jefferson and Adams in 1826.

By contrast, John Adams' tomb in Quincy bears only his name.

The tombs of Jefferson and Adams sum up how historians have viewed the two men. In the 21st century, however, Jefferson's reputation has suffered because he kept slaves all his life. Similarly, Adams' reputation has also been reviewed. In particular, he has been praised for his willingness in 1800 to risk personal unpopularity in order to avoid full-scale war with France.

WAR: British troops burn the White House in Washington, D.C., during the War of 1812.

Changing Political World

By the time Jefferson and Adams died, many of the issues they had fallen out about had disappeared. The last tensions between Britain and the United States had led to the War of 1812 (1812–1814). After that, however, the two countries enjoyed permanent peace. In France, meanwhile, the revolution had ended and the monarchy was back in power. Thanks partly to Jefferson and Adams, the United States was still on good terms with both France and Britain.

> "It is a great day. Thomas Jefferson survives."

John Adams on his deathbed, but Jefferson had died hours earlier.

JUDGMENT

THOMAS JEFFERSON Vs. JOHN ADAMS

Thomas Jefferson has long been respected as the author of the Declaration of Independence, but more recently his reputation has been criticized.

* **Jefferson helped begin the idea that each state has its own rights. A state could reject laws it thought went against the Constitution. Later in the 19th century, the Southern states used this argument to claim they could reject a ban on slavery.**

* **Jefferson kept slaves for his whole life. This seems to go against his statement that all men are born equal.**

* **Jefferson created a form of democracy that allowed the United States to create its own identity free from the rule of Britain.**

Little attention was paid to the achievements of John Adams until the 21st century. Today, he is one of the most admired of all American presidents.

*** Of the first ten presidents, only Adams and his son, John Quincy Adams, did not own slaves.**

*** Adams has always been a celebrated figure in his hometown, Boston, and across Massachusetts.**

*** Adams is one of the presidents we know best, thanks to his letters to his wife, Abigail, and to Thomas Jefferson.**

*** Adams managed to avoid full-scale war during tension and conflict with both Britain and France.**

TIMELINE

The early friendship between Thomas Jefferson and John Adams lasted well over a decade before political differences made them rivals who had no contact for some 20 years.

1775

Americans Revolt
On April 19, 1775, American Patriots fought British soldiers at the Battle of Lexington and Concord, beginning the Revolutionary War.

First Meeting
Thomas Jefferson and John Adams meet for the first time at the Second Continental Congress in Philadelphia.

1776

Draft Declaration
Thomas Jefferson drafts the Declaration of Independence, aided by John Adams and Benjamin Franklin. The document is adopted on July 4.

1785

In Europe
John Adams moves to London as US ambassador. He and his wife, Abigail, frequently see Thomas Jefferson, then living in Paris, France.

1789

Revolution in France
Republicans topple the monarchy in France, which enters years of violence. While Jefferson supports the Revolution, Adams is opposed to it.

1791

The Rights of Man
When a publisher prints Jefferson's thoughts about the French Revolution, which criticize Adams, Adams takes offense and their friendship weakens.

Jay's Treaty
John Jay makes a treaty to regularize relations between the United States and Britain. While Adams supports the treaty, Jefferson believes it unfairly favors Britain.

French Rebellion
In July, Congress rejects treaties with France made before the French Revolution. This begins the Quasi-War, a series of small naval clashes that last until September 1800.

No Second Term
Jefferson defeats Adams in the presidential election; Adams retires to his home. Jefferson serves two terms as president before retiring.

1794 1796 1798 1800 1812

President Adams
John Adams, standing for the Federalists, narrowly defeats Jefferson, the Democratic-Republican candidate, in the presidential election; Jefferson reluctantly becomes vice president.

Gagging Laws
Jefferson and the Democratic-Republicans protest against the Alien and Sedition Acts, introduced by Adams to prevent foreign interference in US affairs.

Reconciliation
On January 1, prompted by Benjamin Rush, Adams writes to wish Jefferson a happy new year. Jefferson replies and the two men are reconciled.

GLOSSARY

allegiance Loyalty to a group or cause.

allies Countries or individuals who agree to act together to achieve a shared goal.

ambassador An official who represents his or her country in a foreign country.

anarchy A state of disorder caused by the lack of authority or rules.

aristocracy The nobles who formed an elite in some societies .

broadside A large sheet of paper printed on one side, often displayed as a poster.

cabinet The group of senior ministers who control a government's policies.

colony An area or country settled by and governed by another country.

commiserate To express sympathy with someone.

corrupted Acting dishonestly in return for personal gain.

debt A sum of money that is owed to someone else.

Democratic-Republicans A political party that emphasized the importance of states' rights.

diplomatic relations The normal conduct of relations between two countries through their official representatives.

dynasty A series of people from the same family who play important roles in politics or business.

executive The part of a government that is responsible for putting laws into action.

federal Related to the central government in a country made up of units such as states.

Federalists A political party that supported a strong central, or federal, government.

fluent Able to express oneself easily and effectively.

Founding Fathers Members of the convention who created the US Constitution.

guarantee To promise something with certainty that it will happen.

harass To put pressure on someone or intimidate them.

idealist A person who is guided more by ideas than by practical considerations.

judiciary The part of a government that is responsible for the legal system.

landslide A large majority of votes for one party or candidate in an election.

legislature The branch of a government that is responsible for making or changing laws.

nullify To make something no longer effective.

principles The fundamental values by which an individual chooses to live.

Puritan Related to a branch of Christianity that emphasized simplicity and modesty.

realist Someone who deals with things as they are, not with how they would ideally be.

reconciliation The restoration of friendly relations between people.

widower A man whose wife has died.

FOR FURTHER INFORMATION

Books

Elston, Heidi M.D. *John Adams: 2nd President of the United States*. United States Presidents. Edina, MN: ABDO Publishing Co, 2009.

Elston, Heidi M.D. *Thomas Jefferson: 3rd President of the United States*. United States Presidents. Edina, MN: ABDO Publishing Co, 2009.

Gould, Jane H. *John Adams.* Junior Graphic Founding Fathers. New York: PowerKids Press, 2012.

Gregory, Josh. *The French Revolution*. Cornerstones of Freedom. New York: Children's Press, 2014.

Meacham, Jon. *Thomas Jefferson: President and Philosopher*. New York: Crown Books for Young Readers, 2014.

Websites

http://www.history.com/topics/us-presidents/john-adams/
History.com page about John Adams, with videos and links to other pages.

http://www.history.com/topics/us-presidents/thomas-jefferson
A similar page about Jefferson.

https://www.whitehouse.gov/1600/presidents/johnadams
Biography of John Adams from the White House site.

http://www.monticello.org/
Website of Jefferson's home at Monticello.

https://history.state.gov/milestones/1784-1800/xyz
An account of the Quasi-War from the Department of State.

https://history.state.gov/milestones/1784-1800/french-rev
Department of State page about American reaction to the French Revolution.

Publisher's note to educators and parents: Our editors have carefully reviewed these websites to ensure that they are suitable for students. Many websites change frequently, however, and we cannot guarantee that a site's future contents will continue to meet our high standards of quality and educational value. Be advised that students should be closely supervised whenever they access the Internet.

INDEX